PIANO • VOCAL • GUITAR

GREATEST HITS
VOLUME 1

2 PRAYIN' FOR DAYLIGHT

10 I'M MOVIN' ON

15 THESE DAYS

24 I MELT

30 MAYBERRY

36 FEELS LIKE TODAY

41 BLESS THE BROKEN ROAD

48 FAST CARS AND FREEDOM

55 SKIN (SARABETH)

61 WHAT HURTS THE MOST

67 MY WISH

76 STAND

81 LIFE IS A HIGHWAY

ISBN 978-1-4234-6832-5

7777 W. BLUEMOUND RD. P.O. BOX 13819 MILWAUKEE, WI 53213

For all works contained herein:
Unauthorized copying, arranging, adapting, recording, Internet posting, public performance,
or other distribution of the printed music in this publication is an infringement of copyright.
Infringers are liable under the law.

Visit Hal Leonard Online at
www.halleonard.com

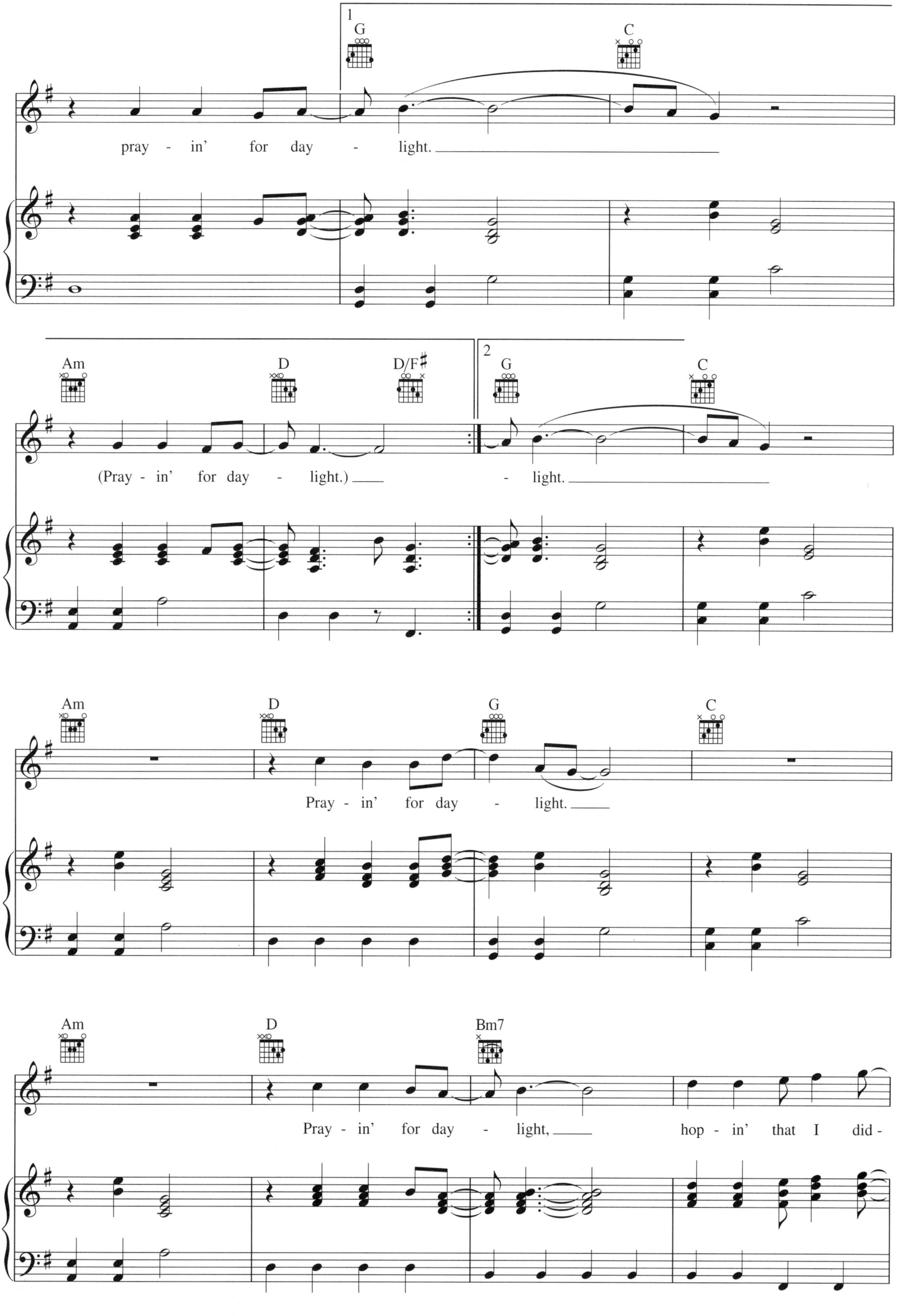
1
G
C
pray - in' for day - light.
Am
D
D/F#
2
G
C
(Pray - in' for day - light.)
- light.
Am
D
G
C
Pray - in' for day - light.
Am
D
Bm7
Pray - in' for day - light,
hop - in' that I did -

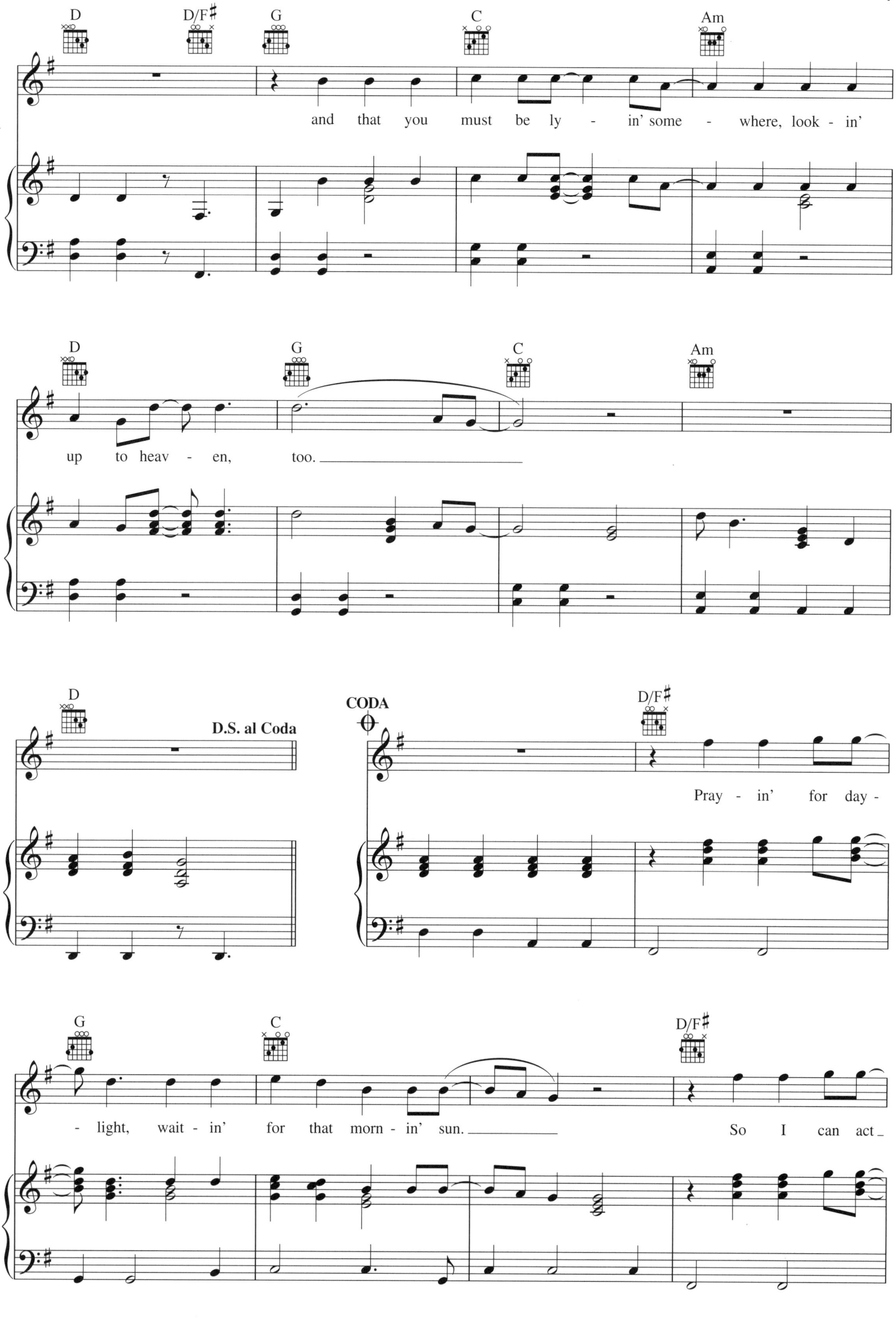
D D/F# G C Am
and that you must be ly - in' some - where, look - in'
D G C Am
up to heav - en, too.
D
D.S. al Coda
CODA
D/F#
Pray - in' for day -
G C D/F#
- light, wait - in' for that morn - in' sun.
So I can act

12

THESE DAYS

Words and Music by DANNY WELLS,
STEVE ROBSON and JEFFREY STEELE

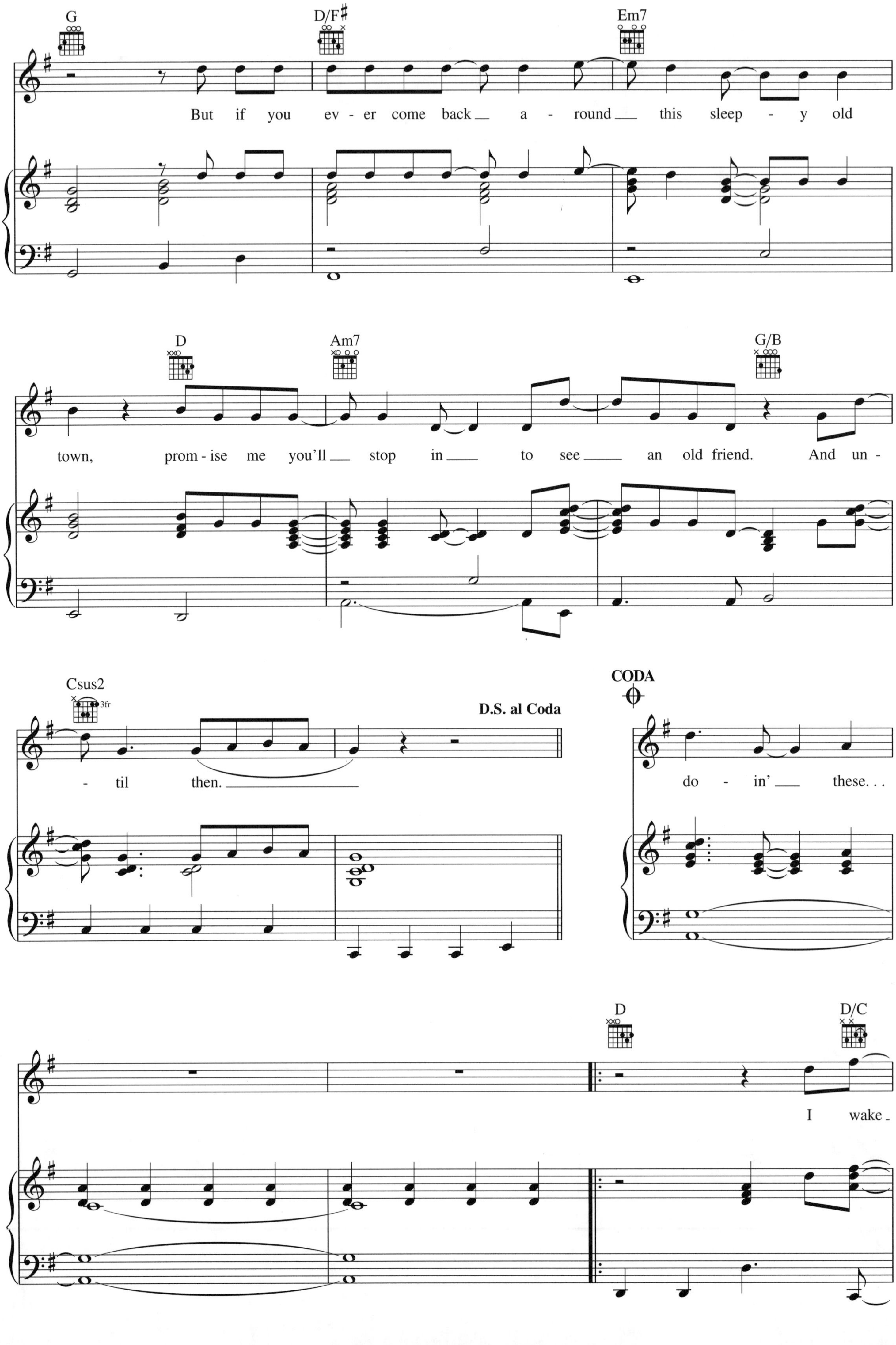
G
D/F#
Em7
But if you ev - er come back a - round this sleep - y old
D
Am7
G/B
town, prom - ise me you'll stop in to see an old friend. And un -
Csus2
3fr
D.S. al Coda
- til then.
CODA
do - in' these...
D
D/C
I wake

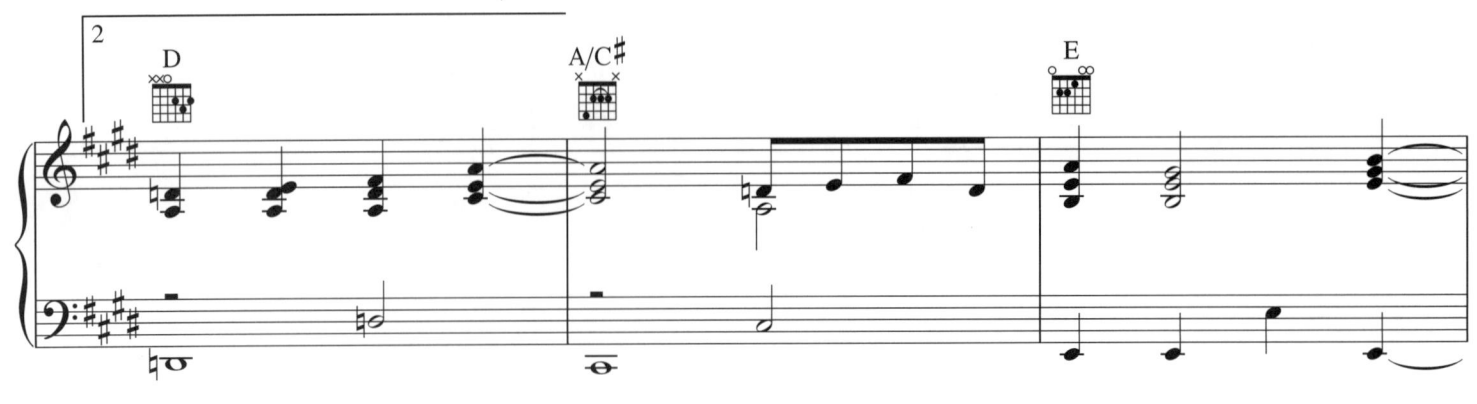
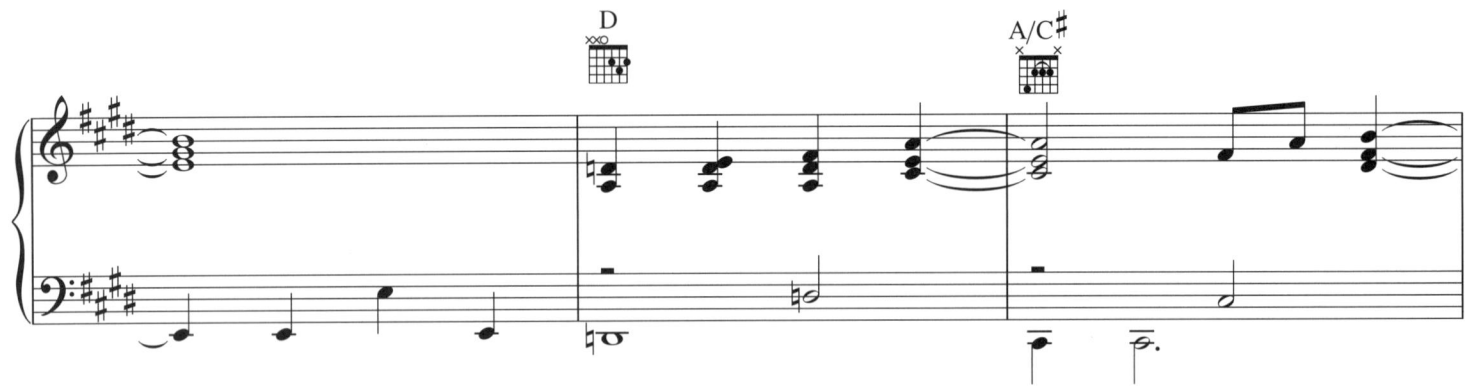

I melt

Ev - 'ry time you

MAYBERRY

Words and Music by
ARLOS DARRELL SMITH

* Recorded a half step higher.

Copyright © 2002 by Peertunes, Ltd. and Good Ole Delta Boy Music
All Rights Administered by Peertunes, Ltd.
International Copyright Secured   All Rights Reserved

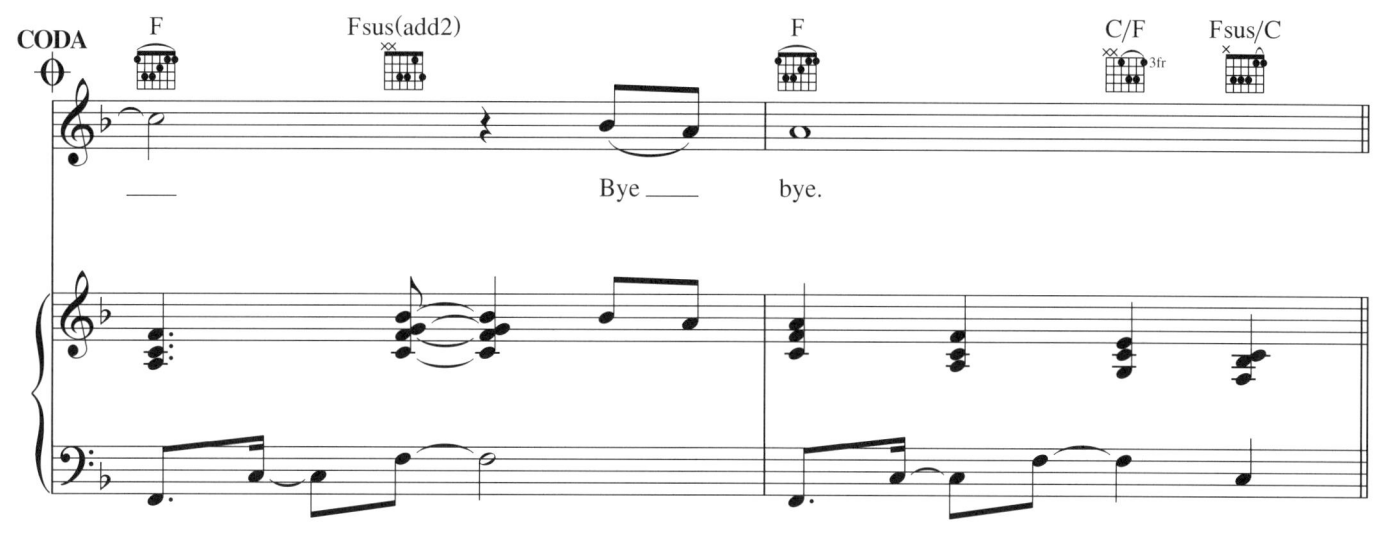
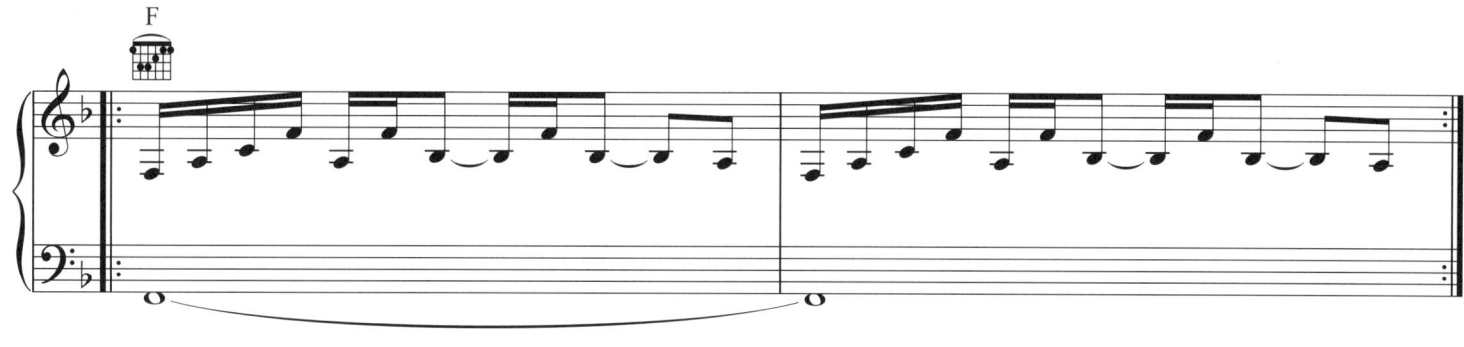

FEELS LIKE TODAY

Words and Music by WAYNE HECTOR
and STEVE ROBSON

*Recorded a half step lower.

Copyright © 2004 RONDOR MUSIC (LONDON) LTD. and UNIVERSAL MUSIC PUBLISHING LTD.
All Rights for RONDOR MUSIC (LONDON) LTD. in the U.S. and Canada Controlled and Administered by ALMO MUSIC CORP.
All Rights for UNIVERSAL MUSIC PUBLISHING LTD. in the U.S. and Canada Controlled and Administered by UNIVERSAL - POLYGRAM INTERNATIONAL PUBLISHING, INC.
All Rights Reserved   Used by Permission

BLESS THE BROKEN ROAD

Words and Music by MARCUS HUMMON,
BOBBY BOYD and JEFF HANNA

Copyright © 1994 by Universal Music - Careers, Floyd's Dream Music and Jeff Diggs Music
All Rights for Floyd's Dream Music Administered by Universal Music - Careers
All Rights for Jeff Diggs Music Administered by Bug Music
International Copyright Secured All Rights Reserved

FAST CARS AND FREEDOM

Words and Music by GARY LEVOX,
WENDELL MOBLEY and NEIL THRASHER

* Recorded a half step higher.

Copyright © 2004 Sony/ATV Music Publishing LLC, Dimensional Music Of 1091, Warner-Tamerlane Publishing Corp., Lexi's Palm Tree Music, Major Bob Music, Inc. and Sweet Summer Music
All Rights on behalf of Sony/ATV Music Publishing LLC Administered by Sony/ATV Music Publishing LLC, 8 Music Square West, Nashville, TN 37203
All Rights on behalf of Lexi's Palm Tree Music Administered by Warner-Tamerlane Publishing Corp.
All Rights on behalf of Sweet Summer Music Administered by Kobalt Music Publishing America, Inc.
International Copyright Secured   All Rights Reserved

see _____ what I _____ see when it's gone. _____
front _____ porch, lookin' just like that. _____

I see a dust _____ trail followin' an old _____ red Nova,

baby blue eyes, _____ your head _____ on my shoulder. _____

Wait, baby, don't move, _____ right there it is. _____ A t-

WHAT HURTS THE MOST

Words and Music by STEVE ROBSON
and JEFFREY STEELE

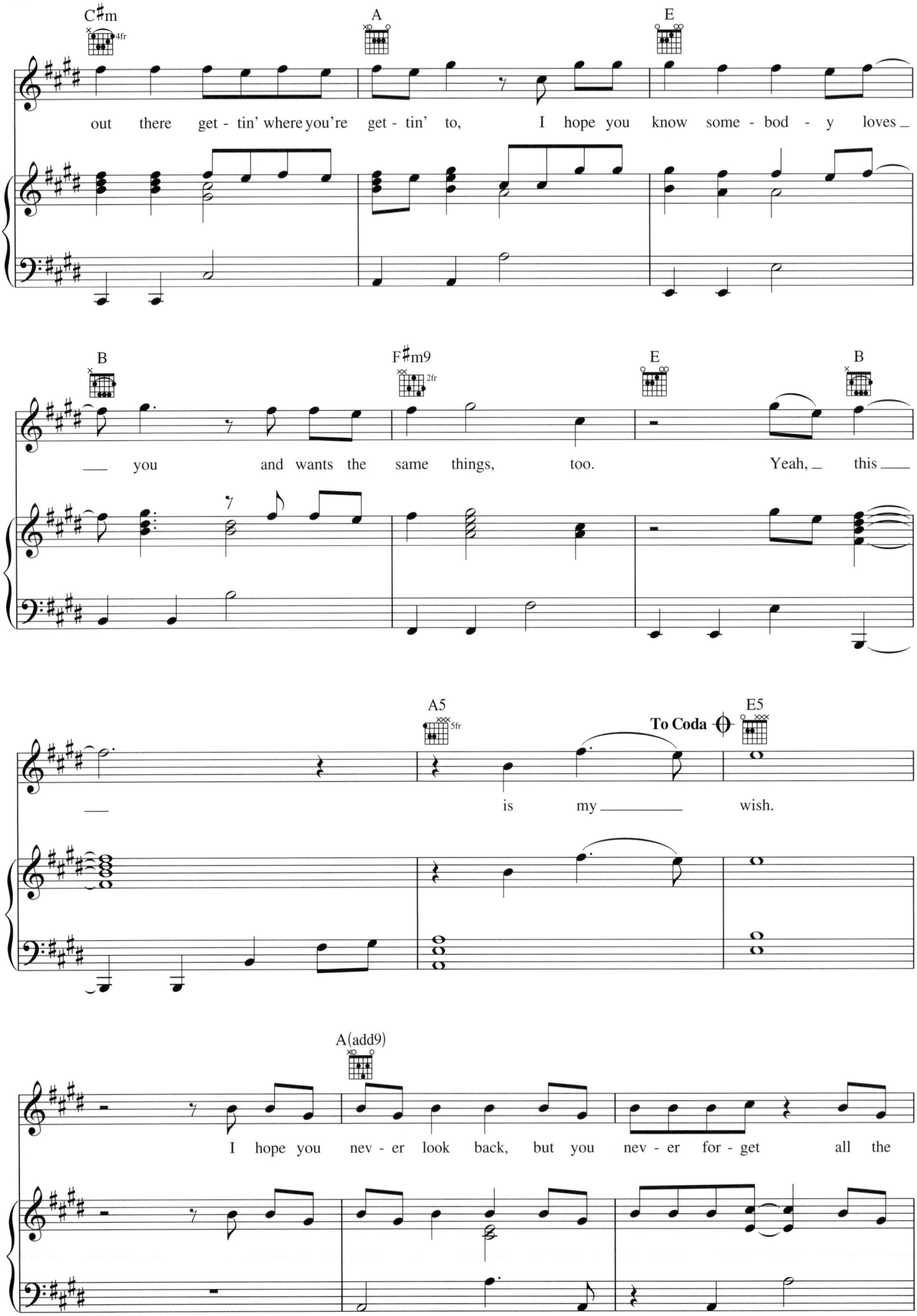
C♯m
4fr
A
E
out there get - tin' where you're get - tin' to, I hope you know some - bod - y loves
B
F♯m9
2fr
E
B
you and wants the same things, too. Yeah, this
A5
5fr
To Coda
E5
is my wish.
A(add9)
I hope you nev - er look back, but you nev - er for - get all the

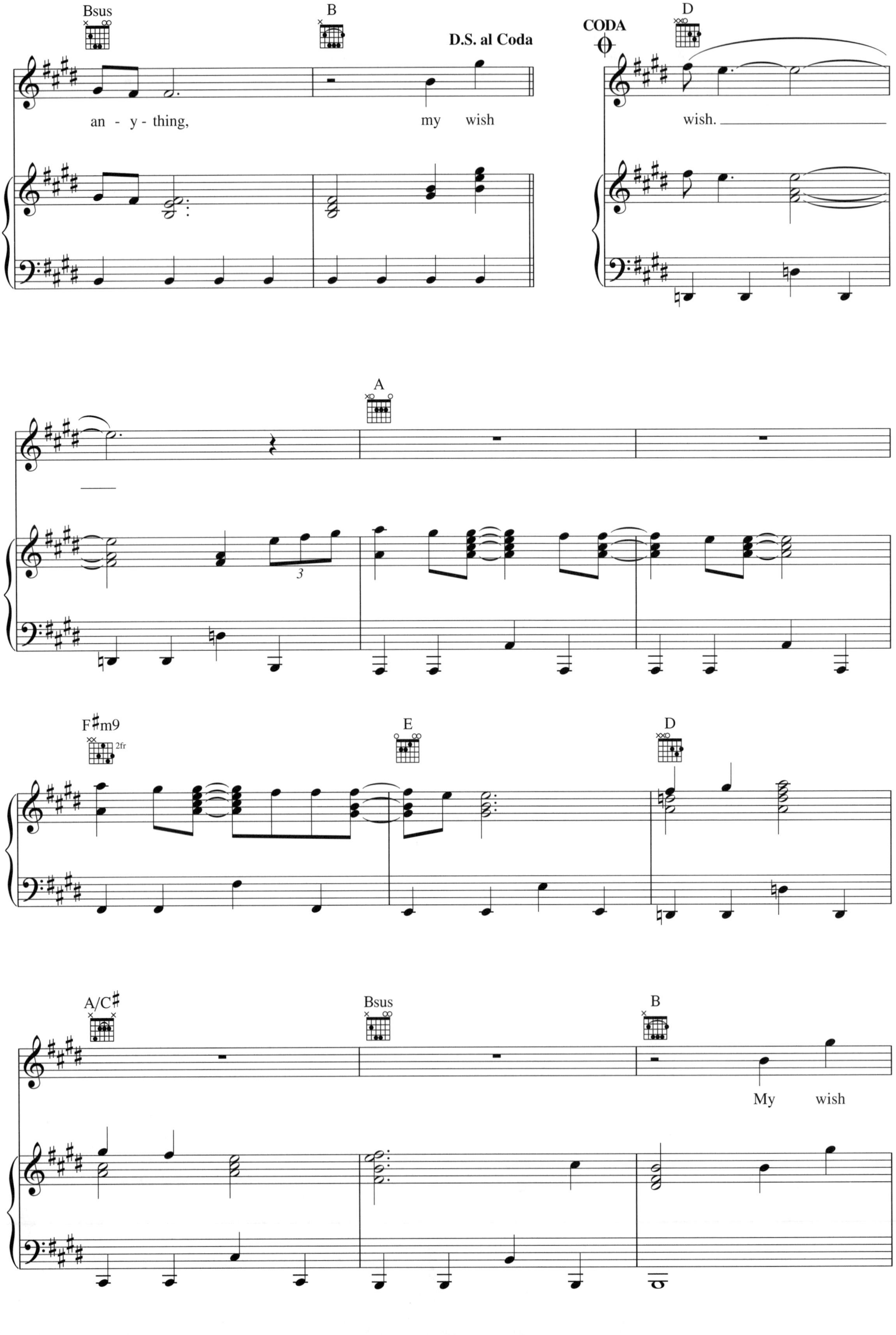
Bsus
B
D.S. al Coda
CODA
D
an - y - thing,
my wish
wish.
3
A
F♯m9
2fr
E
D
A/C♯
Bsus
B
My wish

STAND

Words and Music by BLAIR DALY
and DANNY ORTON

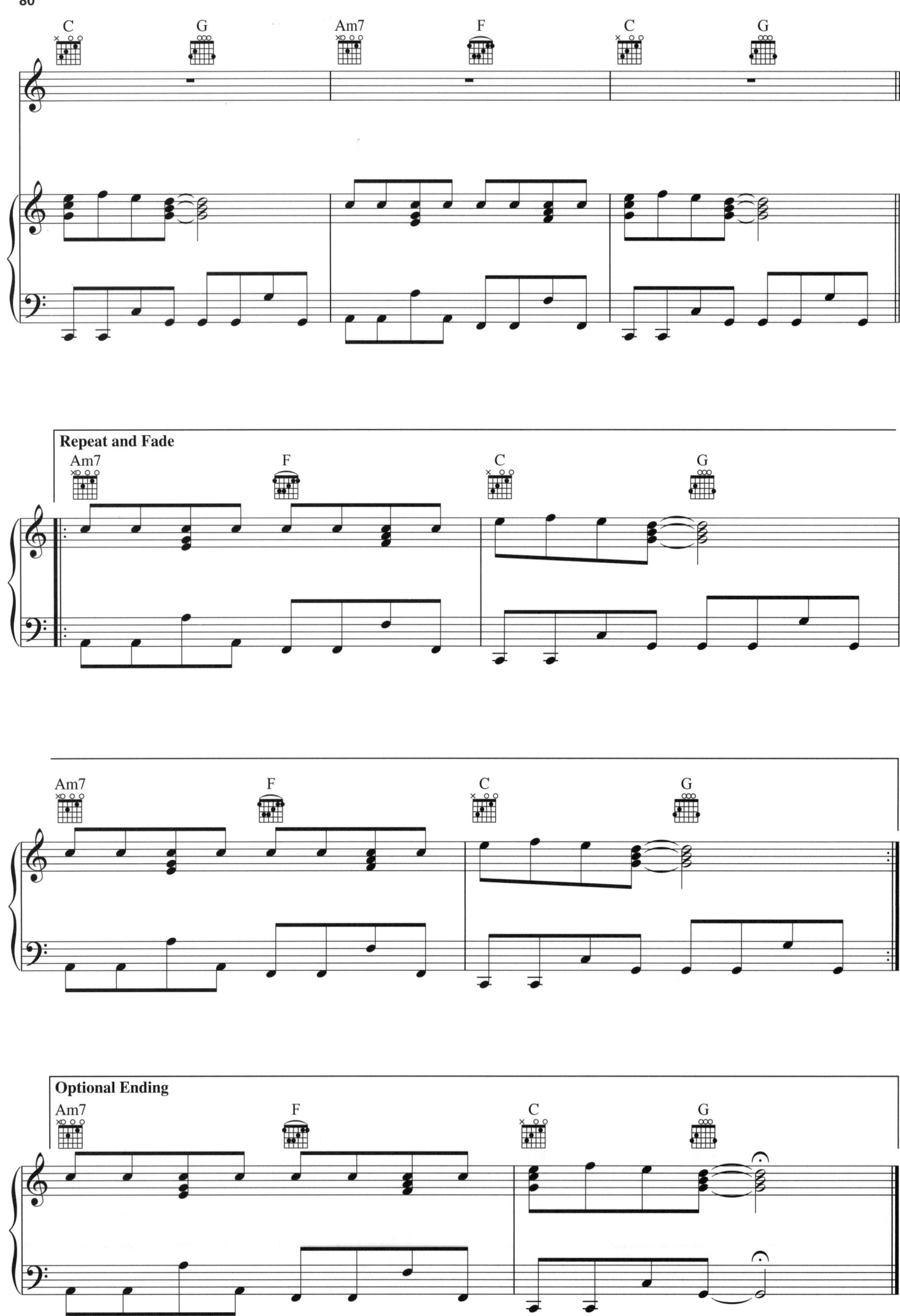

LIFE IS A HIGHWAY

Words and Music by
TOM COCHRANE

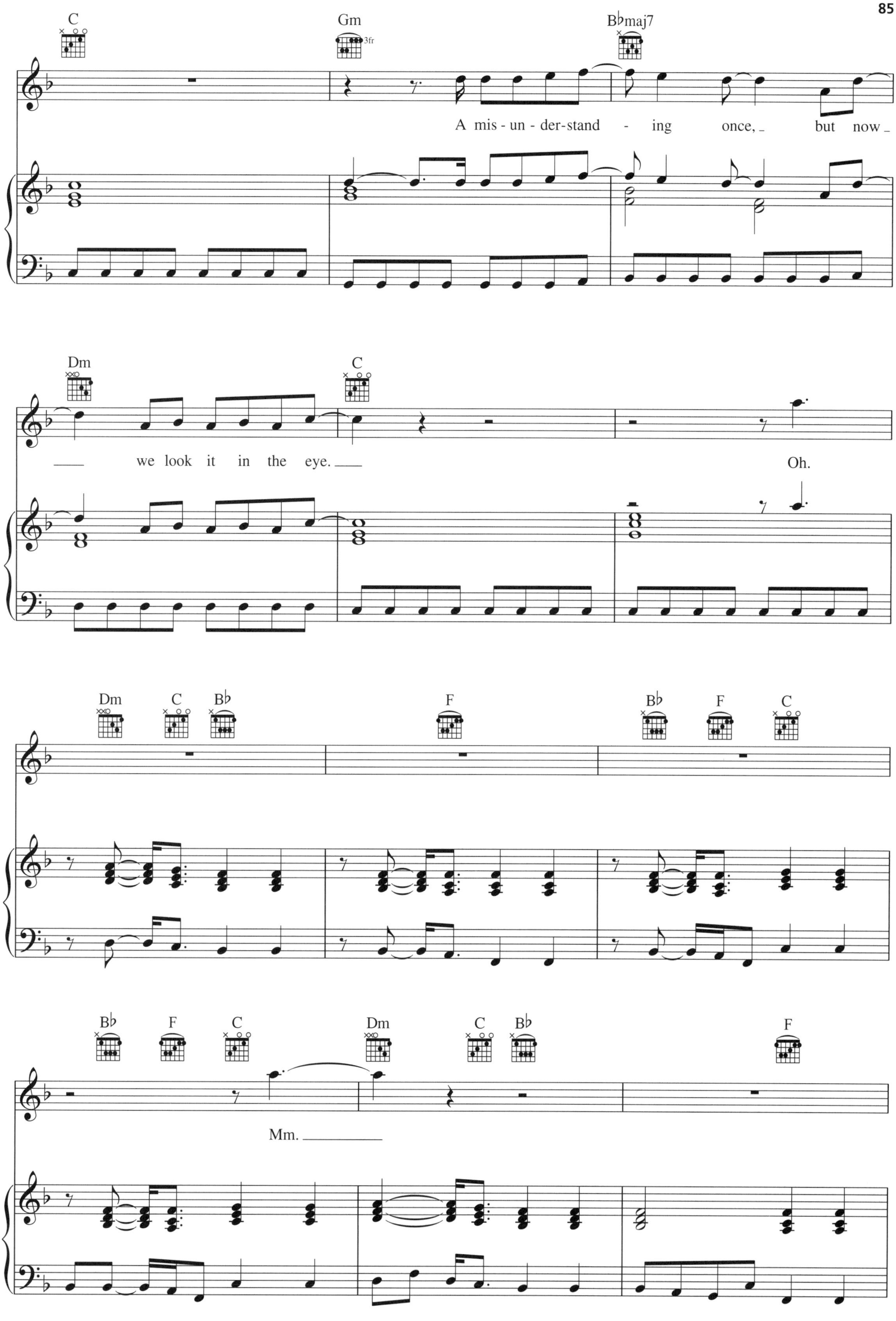
C
Gm
3fr
B♭maj7
A mis - un - der - stand - ing once, but now
Dm
C
we look it in the eye.
Oh.
Dm C B♭
F
B♭ F C
B♭ F C
Dm C B♭
F
Mm.